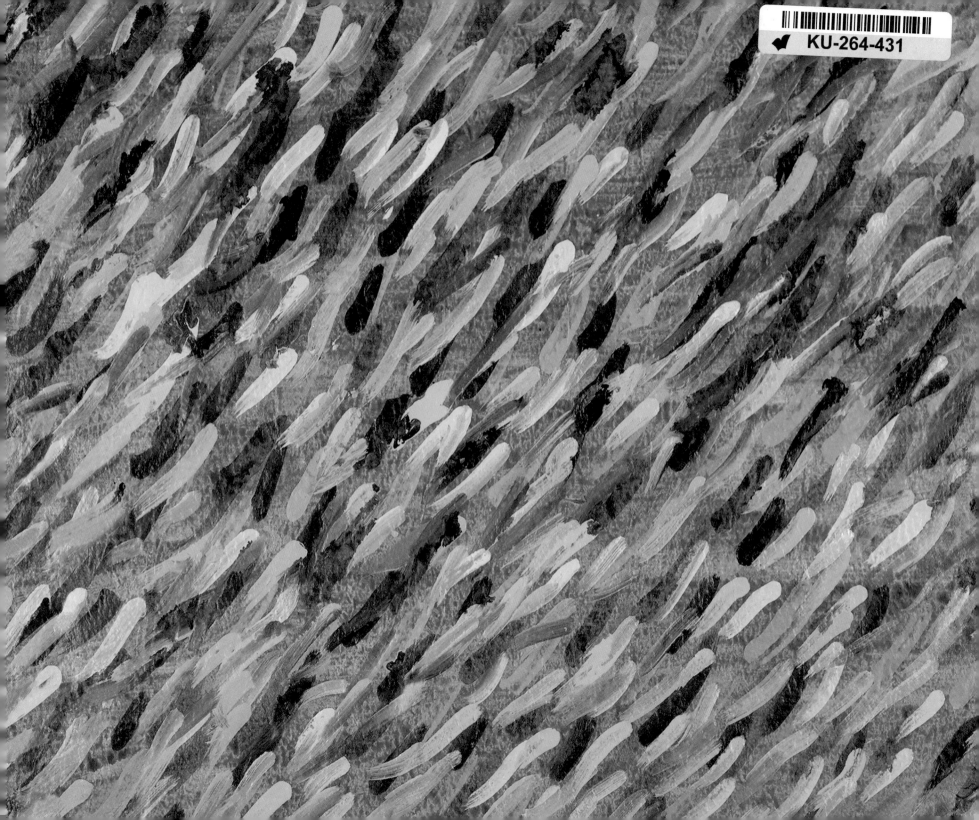

For Fred Rogers

DOES A KANGAROO

Ann Beneduce, Creative Editor

The author and publisher thank Wendy Worth, Curator of Birds
and Small Mammals, Zoo Atlanta, Atlanta, Georgia, for her advice
and comments.

First published in hardback by HarperCollins Publishers, USA in 2000
First published in hardback in Great Britain by Collins in 2000
First published in paperback by Collins Picture Books in 2001
Collins Picture Books is an imprint of the Children's Division, part of
HarperCollins Publishers Ltd.

1 3 5 7 9 10 8 6 4 2
ISBN: 0 00 710616 5

The HarperCollins website address is: www.fireandwater.com

Printed in Great Britain by Scotprint

HAVE A MOTHER, TOO ?

by Eric Carle

Collins

An imprint of HarperCollinsPublishers

YES !

A **KANGAROO** has a mother.
Just like me and you.

Does a lion have a mother, too?

Yes!
A **LION** has a mother.
Just like me and you.

Does a giraffe have a mother, too?

Yes!
A GIRAFFE has a mother.
Just like me and you.

Does a penguin have a mother, too?

Yes!
A **PENGUIN** has a mother.
Just like me and you.

Does a swan have a mother, too?

Yes!
A SWAN has a mother.
Just like me and you.

Does a fox have a mother, too?

Yes!
A **FOX** has a mother.
Just like me and you.

Does a dolphin have a mother, too?

Yes!
A DOLPHIN has a mother.
Just like me and you.

Does a sheep have a mother, too?

Yes!

A SHEEP has a mother.

Just like me and you.

Does a bear have a mother, too?

Yes!
A **BEAR** has a mother.
Just like me and you.

Does an elephant have a mother, too?

Yes!
An **ELEPHANT** has a mother.
Just like me and you.

Does a monkey have a mother, too?

Yes!
A **MONKEY** has a mother.
Just like me and you.

And do animal mothers love their babies?

YES ! YES ! Of course they do.

Animal mothers love their babies,
just as yours loves you.

Names of animal babies, parents, and groups in this book

Kangaroo A baby kangaroo is a **joey**. Its mother is a **flyer** and its father is a **boomer**. A group of kangaroos is a **troop** or a **mob** or a **herd**.

Lion A baby lion is a **cub**. Its mother is a **lioness** and its father is a **lion**. A group of lions is a **pride**.

Giraffe A baby giraffe is a **calf**. Its mother is a **cow** and its father is a **bull**. A group of giraffes is a **tower** or a **herd**.

Penguin A baby penguin is a **chick**. Its mother is a **dam** and its father is a **sire**. A group of penguins is a **colony** or a **parade**.

Swan A baby swan is a **cygnet**. Its mother is a **pen** and its father is a **cob**. A group of swans is a **wedge** or a **herd**.

Fox A baby fox is a **cub** or a **pup**. Its mother is a **vixen** and its father is a **dog fox**. A group of foxes is a **pack** or a **skulk**.

Dolphin A baby dolphin is a **calf**. Its mother is a **cow** and its father is a **bull**. A group of dolphins is a **school** or a **pod**.

Sheep A baby sheep is a **lamb**. Its mother is a **ewe** and its father is a **ram**. A group of sheep is a **flock**.

Bear A baby bear is a **cub**. Its mother is a **sow** and its father is a **boar**. A group of bears is a **pack** or a **sloth**.

Elephant A baby elephant is a **calf**. Its mother is a **cow** and its father is a **bull**. A group of elephants is a **herd**.

Monkey A baby monkey is an **infant**. Its mother is a **mother** and its father is a **father**. A group of monkeys is a **group** or a **troop** or a **tribe**.

Deer A baby deer is a **fawn**. Its mother is a **doe** and its father is a **buck**. A group of deer is a **herd**.

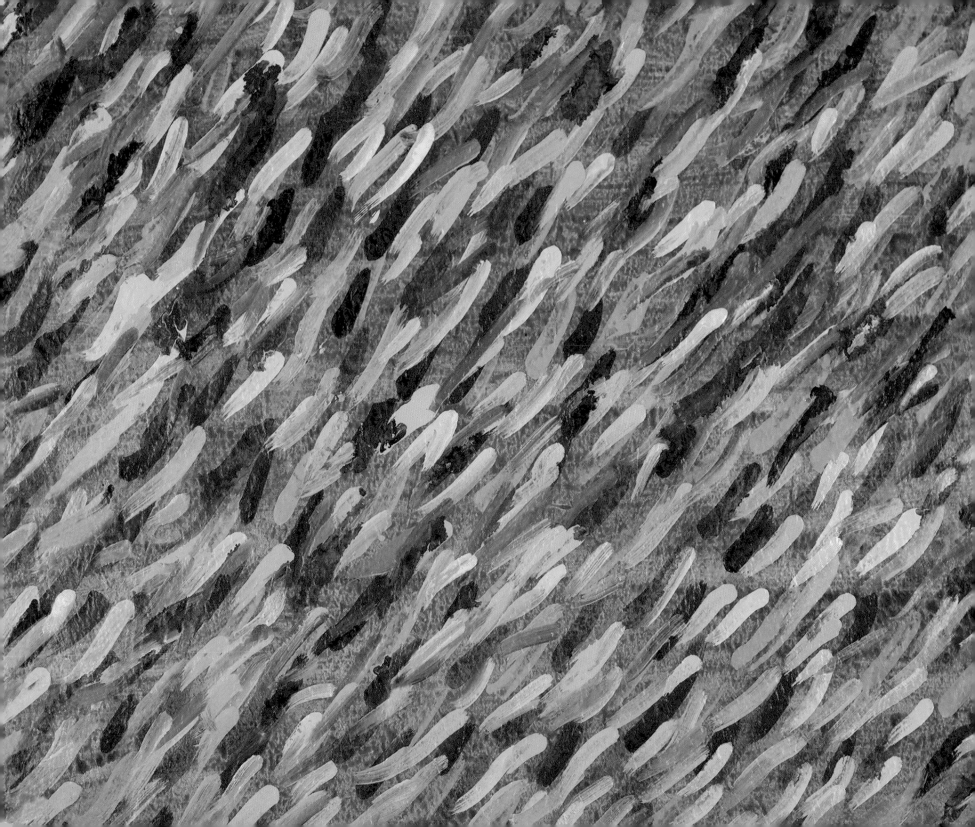

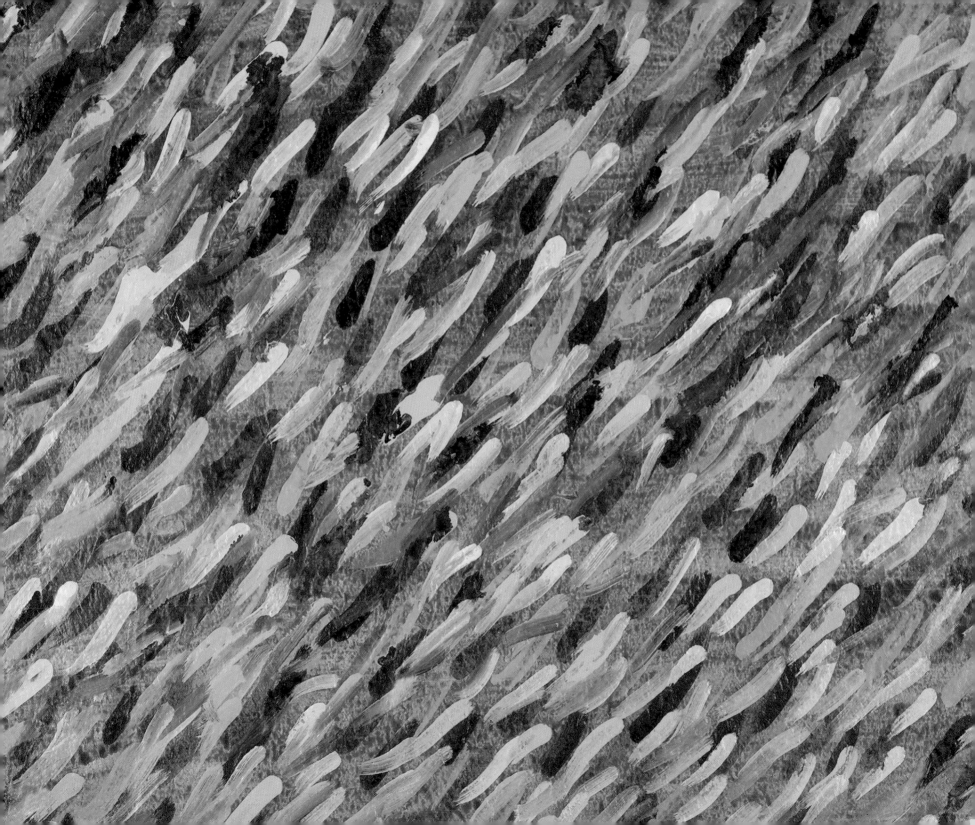